Boeing 737

-100 and -200

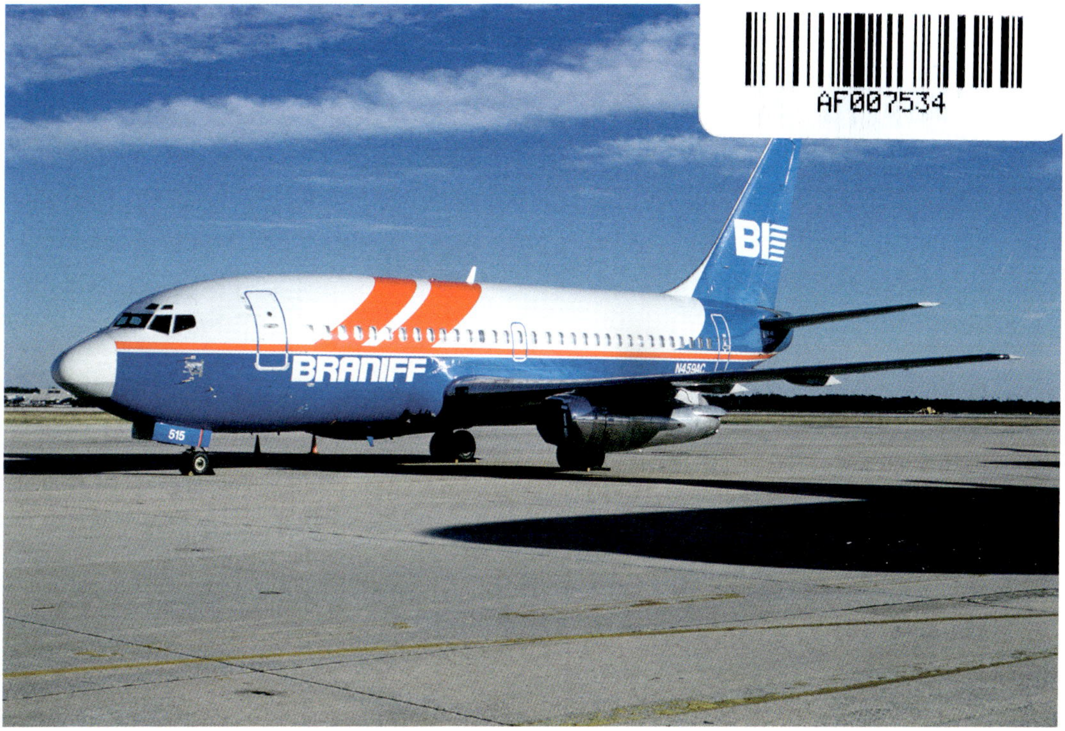

MATT FALCUS

KEY Books

HISTORIC COMMERCIAL AIRCRAFT SERIES, VOLUME 16

Front cover image: GB Airways was a BA franchise partner tasked with providing links to Gibraltar from the UK and North Africa. It would also offer summer charters, with a total of nine 737-200s passing through its ranks on lease during its history. This aircraft, G-DDDV, flew with the airline in 1988 and 1989.

Title page image: Following the demise of the original Braniff International in 1982, some of its assets were acquired to form a new airline, Braniff Inc, which launched in 1984. Initially flying the Boeing 727-200, it also leased ten 737-200s.

Contents page image: Perhaps no other airline has such an association with the Boeing 737 as Southwest Airlines. It began offering low-cost flying with the type in 1979 and still flies a fleet comprising almost 800 of the latest variants today.

Back cover image: Britannia Airways signed a contract to order four (later increasing to five) Boeing 737-200s in February 1966. The first aircraft was delivered from Seattle (via a stop in Goose Bay, Canada) on 8 July 1968, making Britannia the first airline in the UK (and indeed all of Europe) to operate the type.

Acknowledgements

My very sincere thanks to the photographers who have kindly supplied incredible images of the 737 for use in this book, most notably Dirk Grothe, Mehrad Watson and Robbie Shaw. My thanks also to the team at Key Publishing for its support.

Published by Key Books
An imprint of Key Publishing Ltd
PO Box 100
Stamford
Lincs PE9 1XQ

www.keypublishing.com

The right of Matt Falcus to be identified as the author of this book has been asserted in accordance with the Copyright, Designs and Patents Act 1988 Sections 77 and 78.

Copyright © Matt Falcus, 2023

ISBN 978 1 80282 718 7

All rights reserved. Reproduction in whole or in part in any form whatsoever or by any means is strictly prohibited without the prior permission of the Publisher.

Typeset by SJmagic DESIGN SERVICES, India.

Contents

Introduction		4
Chapter 1	Developing the Boeing 737	6
Chapter 2	Boeing 737-100	11
Chapter 3	Boeing 737-200	16
Chapter 4	European Operators	22
Chapter 5	North American Operators	50
Chapter 6	South and Central American Operators	64
Chapter 7	Asian and Australasian Operators	70
Chapter 8	African and Middle East Operators	77
Chapter 9	Boeing 737-100 and -200 Today	86
Chapter 10	Technical Specifications	93
Bibliography		95

Introduction

The influence that the Boeing 737 has had on commercial aviation cannot be understated. Still in production today, it is one of the highest-selling airliners of all time, with tens of thousands of airframes built. Not without its controversies, the 737 has nevertheless flown millions of passengers and miles and evolved through many different variants in its 50-year history.

To tell the story of the 737, we need to go back to the earliest days of jet travel in the 1960s, and the successful designs produced by Boeing in Seattle. With the 727 already proving a hit, the manufacturer saw potential for a smaller aircraft with similar design and characteristics that could satisfy so-called 'thinner' routes with fewer passengers, which so far had been the domain of the previous generation of piston airliners. Although other manufacturers were already producing similar aircraft, pioneering Boeing felt it could compete for a meaningful number of sales.

The talented designers, including Joe Sutter, who would go on to manage the design team on the 747, came up with an optimum configuration that eventually departed from the design of the T-tail and rear-mounted engines of the 727. However, to save time when competitors at British Aircraft Corporation

The first Boeing 737 in flight. (Boeing)

Introduction

(BAC), Douglas and Fokker were already working on similar airliners, the engineers at Boeing managed to retain 60 per cent of the structure and systems of the 707 and 727, including the fuselage cross-section and cockpit shape.

Keen to gain big name customers for its new design, Boeing was persuaded to add to the 737's offering before the first aircraft had even been delivered by proposing a larger version. United Airlines was keen to buy 40 of the type, but the company required greater passenger capacity. Therefore, just as Lufthansa was about to receive its first 737-100 in December 1967, becoming the first operator of the new airliner, Boeing was already building the larger -200 model, which would soon become the standard production model until later variants were developed in the 1980s.

To the casual observer, it may be assumed that Boeing immediately went on to great success with the 737-200, which followed straight after the -100, especially given the status and number of sales we see today. However, this was not the case. Orders were sluggish to start with, and production nearly dried up until a resurgence in the 1970s revitalised the aircraft. If it hadn't, we might have a different story to tell today, and successive variants such as the 'Classic' 737-300/400/500 models, the Next Generation 737-600/700/800/900s, and today's 737 MAX variants might not have seen the light of day.

This book tells the story of the genesis of the Boeing 737, and the far reach these early airframes saw around the world is illustrated by the liveries of countless airlines and operators over the years. With hundreds of different operators of the 737-100 and -200, it is not possible to include every one, but by showcasing some of the most notable and interesting examples by each region of the world, it will hopefully demonstrate the history and reach this successful airliner has had.

Even today, the 737-200 is active and going strong in some specialised roles – a true testament to its capabilities and design. The book ends with a look at some of those current operators flying these aircraft today.

Chapter 1

Developing the Boeing 737

The aviation industry, at the time of the Boeing 737's inception, was in a competitive and evolving state. The era of jet air travel had begun in the late 1940s with de Havilland's Comet, which was followed soon after by more early generation airliners. Boeing had little inclination to join the civilian market at the time and was busily employed developing military jet aircraft. This did, however, lead to an opportunity to develop a tanker and transport aircraft for the US Air Force (USAF), which would eventually be known as the KC-135. As a means of offsetting the production costs of this enterprise, Boeing looked at developing a civilian variant capable of carrying passengers. The result was the model 367-80, later to become the Boeing 707 – an airliner that quickly captured the interest of the world's airlines (alongside the Douglas DC-8) and sold well.

Having quickly found its feet in the passenger market once again (the manufacturer had previously enjoyed some early success with piston types such as the Boeing 247 airliner), Boeing went on to develop the 727 to satisfy the medium-haul market. This T-tail airliner was, like most aircraft around the world at the time, built to the specifications of target customer airlines and proved an incredibly

The Boeing 737-100 prototype on the ground at Renton, near Seattle. (Aero Icarus Collection)

capable and well-liked aircraft. It covered the 100–160 passenger capacity range over two variants of different sizes. The 727 launched in 1960 and entered service two years later, with the stretched -200 model arriving in 1967.

In France, Sud Aviation had built the world's first twin-engine jet aircraft, the Caravelle. It first flew in 1955 and introduced the idea of rear-mounted engines and a T-tail design. Its success led to rival manufacturer BAC proposing its own very similar design, the One-Eleven. Launched in 1961, it first flew in 1963 and entered service with British United Airways on 22 January 1965.

Similarly, Boeing's biggest competitor in the US market, Douglas, had launched its own version of this now common design, the DC-9. Like the One-Eleven, it featured a T-tail design, twin rear-mounted engines and had a capacity for around 80–90 passengers. It first flew in February 1965 and entered service with Delta Air Lines later that year.

Boeing, having launched the 727 with good success, felt that entering the market for a smaller jet airliner might be an expensive and difficult process, but could also be essential to the company's survival and reputation. This was especially true given Douglas and BAC were looking at stretched versions of the DC-9 and One-Eleven, which would take them closer to the 727's capacity and potentially reduce Boeing's market share. Thus, the 737 project was born.

Searching for a Launch Customer

In order to justify taking the leap into producing a brand new airliner, Boeing needed to search for potential customers who would be interested in ordering the type. As a natural first step, all of the major US and European carriers would need to be courted and sold the benefits of this new type, and so a list of target buyers was drawn up.

Some of these airlines had already ordered the rival types, such as Delta with the DC-9 and American Airlines with the One-Eleven. However, United Airlines and Eastern, which were both launch customers for the 727, were seen as key targets. United had a small fleet of older Caravelles, and Eastern had yet to order a smaller jet airliner.

In Europe, Lufthansa was also seen as a target, having yet to order a smaller jet to complement its 707 and 727 fleets and replace older propliners. Meanwhile, Ansett-ANA in Australia had also shown interest in the new airliner.

At this stage, the exact specifications of the aircraft were very fluid and changing regularly, often in response to discussions with airlines, which each had a preference over capacity, range and other characteristics. The initial requirement for a 50–60 passenger capacity had soon grown to 80, and with Lufthansa emerging as the most likely first customer, this was increased to 100 at the company's request.

Satisfied with this, and other specifications, an order for 21 Boeing 737s was received from Lufthansa on 19 February 1965. The airline had briefly considered ordering the Douglas DC-9 when Boeing was still wavering on committing to the 737, but by mutual agreement its order was the catalyst to ensure the 737 would be built.

United Airlines would be the next to commit to an order, but only once its particular capacity requirements had been met. To meet this request, Boeing engineers proposed a stretch in the fuselage length by 193cm (76in) to accommodate 112 passengers. United's order for 40 of what would become the 737-200 was placed on 5 April 1965.

Design Specifications

Given the go-ahead for the new aircraft, the team at Boeing took the sensible approach of designing the 737 with as much commonality to the 727 as possible in order to save time and costs. In fact, as previously mentioned, some 60 per cent of the parts used in the 737 are common to the 727, meaning they were readily available and already in production thanks to the larger sibling.

With its smaller size, only two engines were required to power the 737, and early investigations into placement of these saw Boeing discount mounting them on the rear fuselage (like the 727, as well as the DC-9 and One-Eleven) and instead place them underneath the wings.

The trend at the time was for a T-tail design for the rear tailplane, as seen on the 727 and rival types, and first pioneered by the Caravelle. However, with no rear-mounted engines, and following aerodynamic testing, a horizontal stabiliser was positioned at the base of the vertical fin instead.

This interesting departure from the common design characteristics of the day, seen in US, British, French and even Soviet designs, meant the 737 was considered unusual at the time, and even raised some questions over safety. After all, engines slung under the wings meant problems with wheels-up landings and posed a threat due to their proximity to the fuel tanks. It was also felt that a wing devoid of engines was cleaner and more efficient aerodynamically, while the rear-mounted engines took much of the noise away from the cabin.

However, Boeing's design team had come up with its design with plenty of theoretical testing and commercial insight in mind. The finalised configuration for the 737 meant there would be greater space available in the fuselage for seating and other amenities where as rear-mounted engines would have reduced the available area. There was also a saving of 700kg (¾ ton) over the rear-mounted design, meaning greater opportunities for payload. Finally, the provision of a larger vertical tail fin meant that any potential problems with asymmetrical thrust on the loss of a wing-mounted engine in flight were negated.

Engineers work on a Pratt & Whitney JT8D engine. The initial 737 model was powered by the JT8D-7, but later upgrades offered customers improved thrust and noise reductions. (Dirk Grothe)

Internally, the 737 again made use of existing Boeing designs and was almost identical to the 727 with six-abreast seating and the same width and shape. This size of cabin was wider than that of the One-Eleven and DC-9. The seating and many features such as the galley modules were also identical to the 727. Much of the same manufacturing of fuselage sections and components from the 727 could be used on the 737, meaning existing manufacturing lines could be used and far less in the way of training of operatives was required to get the 737 into production.

Passenger entry points were two on either side, with an emergency exit on each side over the wings. Internal airstairs were also offered on any of the doors for airlines that wanted the option for their aircraft to operate independently of airport service vehicles.

The wing of the 737 did build on the success of the highly efficient 727 wing, but the nature of engine mounting beneath the wing did mean some redesign was necessary. The smaller size and proposed daily life of the 737, flying shorter sectors at lower altitudes, also meant some rethinking of the wing's design. Its smaller size meant the 737 wing could be lighter, and yet still strengthened by the position of the engines. Aerodynamic devices such as the flaps and spoilers were common to the 727, however.

Finally, one of the most interesting features of the 737, which is still common in today's MAX variants, is the design of the main landing gear retraction mechanism, which has no doors and simply uses the wheels themselves to form a seal. A weight saving is therefore made in not including doors.

Keen to attract as many potential customers as possible, additional configurations of the aircraft were developed in the early stages of the 737's design process. Boeing offered a Combi variant, which provided a freight door on the forward fuselage and an internal moveable bulkhead that allowed airlines to operate a mixed cargo and passenger combination of varying capacities. An alternative Quick Change variant was also proposed, which could, as the name suggests, be quickly changed between an all-freighter and all-passenger configuration using seats on pallets. Thanks to this foresight, Boeing saw early orders of both variants.

Engines

The engines used on the 737 were essentially the same as those offered on the Boeing 727, across its two variants. The 737's design took the unusual step in mounting its two engines under the wing as a space-saving measure. It also meant that the engines could easily be serviced on the ground at smaller airports without the need for specialist access platforms.

The initial 737-100 model was offered with Pratt & Whitney JT8D-7 engines, delivering 6,350kg (14,000lb) of thrust.

The 737-200 would be powered by JT8D-9 or JT8D-15 engines, with greater thrust and improvements in the noise footprint to satisfy new regulations put into place by the Federal Aviation Administration (FAA). The introduction of noise-absorbing materials and amended engine nacelles to reduce noise became standard from 1973 in the -15 and later engines.

Later, JT8D-9A, -17 and -17R engines were made available to customers for installation on their aircraft, each offering increases in thrust.

Production and Testing

Production of the 737 was carried out in Boeing's complex of sites in the Seattle area. Plant No 2 at Boeing Field, near downtown Seattle, was where the final assembly took place, with early production beginning at Renton, some ten miles away. The first flight was on 9 April 1967.

From 1968, production moved entirely to Renton, where larger facilities were available and a greater number of aircraft in various states of production could be accommodated under one roof. Additional parts and assembly occurred in Wichita, Kansas, and since 1983 fuselage production has also taken there.

The cockpit of the 737 was adapted from those of the 707 and 727, and crews operating those aircraft would have found it very familiar. Like those of its contemporary airliners, the flight deck was a place of dials and switches, with a central column housing throttles for the two engines, along with controls for flaps, trim, spoilers and radio equipment. (Dirk Grothe)

Once complete, these large sections would be transported to Renton by rail – a process that continues to this day with the latest models.

Once an aircraft was mated and all systems installed and tested, it would make its first flight, usually departing from Renton and landing at Boeing Field. Often, the aircraft would be painted at Boeing Field and would then undergo a programme of testing before delivery to its customer airline or operator.

Sales Tours

Keen to boost sales in what was an already crowded market, Boeing sent some of its prototype aircraft on tour to demonstrate the type's abilities to prospective airlines. This mainly took place with the -200 model, and later the Advanced variant, which soon became the standard production model. With slower sales in key markets including Europe and North America, Boeing decided many of the improvements in the Advanced model would appeal, in particular, to airlines in the developing world, where shorter and often unprepared runways would benefit from the aircraft's capabilities and power. Tours of Africa and South America in 1968 yielded various orders, and thanks to the booming holiday industry a number of less obvious airlines such as Britannia Airways soon became early customers and champions of the aircraft.

While some US regional airlines had ordered the aircraft, it would not be until the Airline Deregulation Act of 1978 that significant sales of the 737 were seen in America.

Chapter 2
Boeing 737-100

The design settled on by Boeing and launch customer Lufthansa resulted in the 737-100 model. As mentioned, this was a larger aircraft than first put forward by Boeing in its sales pitches, which had been for a jet airliner with a capacity of 60 to 85 passengers much like the early BAC One-Eleven and Douglas DC-9 models, which Boeing saw as its chief competition. The final specification agreed with Lufthansa saw a fuselage stretch to allow up to 100 passengers to be carried.

Satisfying this first customer was essential to Boeing, which, at this stage, had struggled to attract any of its target airlines to buy this new model. Most had already decided to purchase rival BAC and Douglas aircraft, or France's Sud Aviation Caravelle. Therefore, after protracted discussions with the West German airline, the 737 was launched with an order for a mere 21 aircraft. It was still, at this stage, a potentially expensive gamble for Boeing.

Although the -200 model was developed in tandem with the -100, the -100 was still the first to fly. The prototype was manufactured in record time, thanks to its commonality of parts with the 727, and rolled out of the factory in December 1966.

The 737-100 prototype, with serial N73700, undertook its maiden flight on 9 April 1967, over the skies of Seattle to much media and airline attention. The flight lasted two-and-a-half hours and was crewed by test pilots Lew Wallick and Brien Wygl. The aircraft landed at Paine Field in Everett, to the north of Seattle.

Boeing had filled its production line with successive test aircraft, which allowed the certification process to be undertaken with six active airframes (which included two -200 models). Around 1,300 hours of flight testing were completed, with any problems in handling and performance of the aircraft and its engines noted and worked on by the design and manufacturing teams on the ground.

Some early problems included a worse than expected rate of drag when cruising at high speeds, which was rectified by adding new engine nacelles, and led Boeing to reluctantly strengthen the aircraft's wing spars, adding weight to the airframe and penalties to its performance. The trial-and-error process of refining this took up a lot of the test programme. Testing also included bad weather approaches, with the 737 capable of performing so-called Category II landings, with a decision height of between 30–60m (100–200ft) and a runway visual range of 350–800m (1,200–2,400ft). These conditions had already been met by rival aircraft and were essential if the 737 was to be competitive.

To the relief of all at Boeing, certification of the Boeing 737 was granted by the FAA on 15 December 1967.

The prototype nearing completion in the production hall at Boeing Field in Seattle.

First Deliveries

The first four of Lufthansa's Boeing 737-100 fleet flew as part of the test programme prior to certification, before delivery of the first two – D-ABEB and D-ABEC – in December 1967.

In the 1960s, Lufthansa was a flourishing airline. Free of many of the bounds imposed on it following World War Two, the airline had managed to grow a strong network of domestic and European routes from cities across Germany. As it looked to move into the jet era, older piston airliners such as the Lockheed Constellation were replaced by Boeing 707s and 727s. However, the latter proved overqualified

Above: Lufthansa Boeing 737-130 D-ABEW on the ground at Manchester Airport, UK. Following the introduction of this new aircraft on the airline's domestic network, Lufthansa's early 737s would later be seen on many European routes out of its Frankfurt base.

Left: Ansett New Zealand flew four 737-100s, including three of the prototypes, between 1987–89 (Aero Icarus)

for the domestic network, and it was the 737 that the airline planned to use on these routes, leaving the larger 727s to operate European trunk routes.

The airline inaugurated its Boeing 737 service in February 1968 following a period of crew training in Arizona, where good weather allowed Boeing's pilots to impart their knowledge of this brand-new aircraft to the German pilots who would take it into service. As well as domestic routes including Frankfurt to Berlin or Munich, the -100 would also be used on other short-haul European sectors to London and Paris, for example.

Other 737-100 Operators

United Airlines' request for a 737 model with greater capacity inadvertently proved the early death of the original variant, and only 30 -100 models were ever built. With BAC, Douglas and Sud Aviation all creating larger models of their own twin-jet airliners, and only Fokker promoting a smaller jet airliner in the form of the F28, it appeared that Boeing's earlier plan to compete in the small jet category was not necessary. Instead, something closer in capacity to its popular 727, with all of the benefits and advancements introduced in the 737, was preferred by airlines. Even Lufthansa would later order the -200 to cope with the increased demand it found on its short-haul routes.

Aside from the 22 aircraft built for Lufthansa (one extra was added to its original order), and the prototype, which would later be sold to NASA as a flying laboratory, remaining -100 airframes were ordered by Avianca Colombia (2) and Malaysia-Singapore Airlines (5).

Servicios Aéreos Rutas Oriente, or SARO, was an early low-cost airline based at Monterrey in Mexico. It had a mixed fleet of BAC One-Eleven, Douglas DC-9, Boeing 727 and 737 aircraft, including six -100 models acquired from Continental Airlines. (Aero Icarus)

PEOPLExpress was another operator of the 737-100. In fact, the airline based its launch, in 1981, around the type, which it was able to acquire affordably on the second-hand market having been retired from Lufthansa. Based at Newark airport in New Jersey, PEOPLExpress modelled its operation around that of Laker Airways in the United Kingdom, offering bargain fares on commuter routes. It even offered transatlantic routes when it later acquired Boeing 747s. Struggling financially, PEOPLExpress would merge with Continental Airlines in 1987. Its 737-100s (as well as some -200s) would go on to fly with this airline for a few more years, adding another name to the list of airlines to operate the original 'baby Boeing'.

Built for Lufthansa as D-ABER and delivered in November 1968, the 737-130 pictured here found its way to PEOPLExpress in 1981. It was retired in the early 1990s, following the merger with Continental Airlines.

One of the last -100 models to fly commercially was this example, N708AW, operated by America West Airlines. It wore promotional titles advertising the Phoenix Suns basketball team, which was local to the airline's home base. The aircraft was retired in 1999. (Aero Icarus Collection)

As these early aircraft were replaced by other types, including the larger -200 model, the -100s would all go on to find work with other airlines on the second-hand market. Later companies that flew the 737-100 include Aero Continente, Air Florida, America West Airlines, Ansett New Zealand, Far Eastern Air Transport, Magnicharters, PEOPLExpress (and Continental Airlines following their merger), SARO and Sierra Pacific. Some of Lufthansa's fleet would also go on lease to partner leisure airline Condor during 1969–70.

NASA 515

The prototype is the only 737-100 known to survive today, with all other examples having been scrapped by the early 2000s following retirement. In 1974, this prototype aircraft had come to the end of its useful life with Boeing, but would go on to serve in another important role with the National Aeronautics and Space Administration (NASA).

NASA purchased the aircraft, and it was given the new registration N515NA. It was assigned to the Langley Research Center as a flying laboratory and tasked with many ground-breaking roles looking into aircraft and flight safety issues and new technology to make flying safer and more advanced. Among these were the development of electronic flight displays and the digital cockpits that would start appearing in the early 1980s, as well as Microwave Landing Systems, GPS and other precision guidance, and airborne windshear detection.

Inside, the NASA prototype aircraft were numerous stations for engineers and scientists to perform tasks and monitor systems. In the forward cabin, a second cockpit was also installed where modifications and tests could be carried out without the need to alter the main flight deck at the front of the aircraft.

Having spent many years in this role, where the aircraft was known as NASA 515, this original Boeing 737 was retired to Moses Lake, Washington, in 1997 and kept in a dormant, yet active, condition. It was eventually decided to move the aircraft to the Museum of Flight in Seattle on 21 September 2003. The museum's location at Boeing Field, where the aircraft was built and made the first ever Boeing 737 flight 36 years earlier, was a fitting place for its retirement. Brien Wygle, at the controls for the first flight in April 1967, was a passenger on this final flight. The aircraft is now on display among many other historic aircraft, including the Boeing 727 and 747 prototypes. (NASA)

Chapter 3

Boeing 737-200

Unusually, the -200 and -100 were certified by the FAA on the same day, and the first customer delivery of the -200 took place the day after the first -100 was handed over to Lufthansa.

Although Lufthansa's order saw that capacity raised to a 100 passengers, with a maximum of 112 possible, leading to the 737-100 going into production, Boeing's continued push to attract a big-ticket US carrier led to some misgivings about the suitability of the design. United Airlines, in particular, had shown interest in the 737 from an early stage but felt the capacity of the -100 was too low. Keen to make such an essential sale, Boeing's team agreed to stretch the aircraft by 193cm (76in) by inserting fuselage sections in front of and behind the wing. This allowed the airline to add 12 more passenger seats to the cabin and proved enough to convince United to place an order for 40 aircraft.

Traditionally, airliners had always required at least a three-person crew in the cockpit, and this had been so with the 707 and 727. However, the 737 was planned from the outset to enable airlines to operate with only two crew, as indeed did the rival DC-9 and One-Eleven aircraft, which fell under the weight limit to qualify for two-person crews – a rule which would later be dropped anyway. As United was preparing to bring its 737s into service, the Air Line Pilots Association (ALPA) caused a dispute over the number of crew that were required to operate the new aircraft, insisting on three even though the weight limit requirement was no longer mandated by the government. United (as well as Wien Alaska) wished to fly with only two crew in its 737s, the third pilot being essentially redundant, but this was blocked and fought over bitterly by ALPA with crews striking on the grounds of safety and job security, so early deliveries did have a three-person cockpit.

This was a major blow to Boeing, which suddenly found its aircraft was now less attractive than that of its rivals as it now came with the added running cost of an extra crewmember, undoubtedly causing early sales to suffer. The dispute was rectified by the late 1970s, allowing the 737 to operate with a two-pilot crew as planned, and United quickly modified its early delivery aircraft to remove the third crew position.

United Airlines introduced this popular livery, known as the Saul Bass Tulip scheme, in 1974, for its Boeing 737 fleet. Following the initial order for 40 -200s, United would go on to operate more than 100 of the type in total, before final retirement in 2001.

Disappointing Sales

The dispute over crew members and the late arrival of the 737 to the market when compared to its rivals meant that sales were sluggish to begin with. Despite a strong start in attracting two leading airlines, Lufthansa and United, Boeing was only able to attract one other major US player – Western Airlines. Eastern Airlines, the other US target for the 737, despite already operating the 727, had already opted for the DC-9-30, which was available a year before the 737.

In Europe, many of the other major players such as Alitalia, KLM and Swissair, had opted for the Douglas DC-9, and in Britain the government was still keen on promoting British manufactured types such as the Hawker Siddeley Trident and BAC One-Eleven. Nevertheless, following the 737's entry into service in 1968, Boeing was able to secure orders for around 240 aircraft by the end of the following year. The DC-9, however, had sold twice as many in the same time.

Boeing's sales and marketing teams had also found themselves spread quite thin. It had recently launched the high-profile 747, which was rolled out in September 1968, and which was now taking a lot of attention away from the 737. Boeing had bet the company's future on the success of the giant aircraft. However, healthy sales of its narrowbody fleet would undoubtedly help boost finances and was essential to keep its new airliner alive. Therefore, the sales teams' focus was taken off the 747 project and put into pushing the 737 as hard as they could. Looking for alternative avenues to find orders, the traditional US and Europe markets were put aside, and new territories courted for airlines looking to add new aircraft, particularly in the developing world.

Upgraded Variants

While this work was underway, the design team also set to work on improving the 737-200 model, and providing alternative configurations to suit the needs of a wider range of customers.

The -200 Advanced model was was launched after 135 standard models had been built. This newer aircraft sought to address slight underperformance issues with the launch variant. Whilst slightly heavier than the original -200, the Advanced featured more powerful engines, a greater range through larger fuel tanks, and was able to use smaller runways thanks to redesigned flaps and improved anti-skid brakes, including nose-wheel braking for the first time. Offering these features would mean potential orders from carriers in less developed countries could be found because the 737 would be capable of flying out of shorter and less well-prepared airstrips.

The interior of the 737 was also upgraded, adding overhead bins for luggage and some layout changes. A useful result of this meant a new increased seating capacity of up to 130 passengers in a single-class layout could be achieved. Airlines keen to maximise the potential revenue from their aircraft could now sell more seats per flight and generate a greater income.

For airlines operating into unprepared runways, a gravel kit variant was also offered. This added protection under the nose, and special air vents to deflect stones and debris away from the engines.

Finally, so-called 'hush kits' were added to the 737's engines to reduce the volume of the aircraft at a time when new rules on noise were coming into force in the United States and Europe, forcing many older aircraft types to be retired. As a result, sales success followed with orders coming from various markets around the world, including Africa, Asia and the Middle East.

Around 40 aircraft per year were ordered on average throughout the 1970s. The Advanced model would become the standard 737 variant from the 400th airframe, with no reason for airlines to choose the older, less capable models. To help airlines still flying the original -200 variant, Boeing produced modification kits that could be purchased to transform these aircraft into Advanced models.

All Nippon Airways was the first airline to take delivery of the 737-200 Advanced model in 1971. (Contri/CC2 via Wikimedia Commons)

The 737-200C was a Combi, or combined passenger and cargo model. The launch customer was Wien Air Alaska, which would later become Alaska Airlines. The Combi aircraft was ideal for the varying loads of passengers and cargo carried on its intra-Alaska services flying into often remote airports. Many other operators would order the Combi variant to open up potential side revenues in transporting cargo, particularly in the typically quiet overnight downtime when passenger flights would not usually operate.

The 737-200QC was the Quick Change variant, which could be adapted at speed from an all-cargo freighter to an all-passenger model. Seats would be loaded on pallets and locked into place, meaning the changeover process would be very quick, and again gave airlines the option of flying passengers during the day and freight at night, making the most revenue from the aircraft.

European Breakthroughs

In Europe, the 737 was starting to attract the attention of the growing number of leisure carriers making waves in the Inclusive Tour market. This model of ferrying holidaymakers from Northern Europe to sunnier climes in the Mediterranean was matching increasing demand for foreign trips and the value being offered in the 'package holiday' model.

The first airline to order the 737 for this Inclusive Tour model was Britannia Airways, a carrier that had grown its network on a fleet of Lockheed Constellation and Bristol Britannia types. It had ordered five 737-200s in 1968, taking a step into jet aircraft for the first time. It would follow this up with orders for many more Advanced variants. The 737s were utilised for around 2,500 hours per year, helping offset the costs of acquisition and importing goods into the UK much quicker, and a much-increased winter charter programme allowed it to make money throughout the year, not just in the busy summer months.

Other British leisure carriers including Air Europe, Orion Airways and Dan-Air London would follow, along with Hapag-Lloyd of Germany. All were keen to enjoy the benefits this new aircraft had to offer, even over established jet types such as the BAC One-Eleven and Hawker Siddeley Trident, which had limitations on payload and performance.

Meanwhile, following the merger of British European Airways and British Overseas Airways Corporation (BOAC) in 1974 to create British Airways (BA), the British Department of Trade finally relented on its 'Buy British' stance and allowed a one-off order for 19 737-200 Advanced aircraft in July 1978. This came after a trial lease of aircraft from Transavia in Holland.

Britannia Airways saw a huge increase in demand for package holidays in the 1960s. This was the catalyst for choosing to order jet aircraft to replace slower, less luxurious propeller-driven airliners. The 737 proved a big success and scenes like this were common at airports across Europe, where up to 130 passengers were accommodated on flights to and from holiday destinations.

Dubbed the 'Super 737,' the first of BA's aircraft, G-BGDA, began flying in February 1980 from the airline's London Heathrow base, initially to Brussels, Austria, Scandinavia and Switzerland, but later finding its way on to much of the airline's domestic and European networks.

US Boost in Sales

While US legacy airlines such as American, Continental and Trans World Airlines (TWA) had largely ignored the 737, Boeing was able to attract sales from regional airlines that were upgrading to jet equipment, including from Aloha and Piedmont, and an emerging batch of low-fares carriers such as Air California, Pacific Southwest Airlines and Southwest Airlines. Thanks to the Airline Deregulation Act of 1978, many smaller regional airlines were allowed to expand their networks beyond their home market and into other states. USAir and Frontier Airlines quickly ordered the 737-200, allowing them to bolster their expansion and appear competitive. A relatively low backlog of orders for the 737 enabled Boeing to deliver these new aircraft orders fairly quickly.

Soon, the 737-200 started to become a common sight across America. It was now to be found in the fleets of carriers including Air Florida, Alaska Airlines, America West Airlines, Continental Airlines, Delta Air Lines, Midway Airlines and Pan American. Even American Airlines would briefly operate a small fleet of -100s and -200s acquired through its merger with AirCal in 1987.

Aloha Airlines Boeing 737-297 joined the carrier in 1981 as it expanded its fleet for Hawaiian islands services. The airline was in strong competition with Hawaiian Airlines which itself was upgrading to jet equipment in the form of Douglas DC-9s. This aircraft spent its entire life with the airline, apart from short spells on lease to Pacific Express and AirCal/American Airlines.

Military Variant

The USAF showed interest in the Boeing 737 at an early stage, and in May 1971 placed an order for 19 examples. These would take the military designation T-43 and were based on the 737-200 model, beating off competition from the Douglas DC-9. The type was chosen to operate in the Undergraduate Navigation Training System role, taking the nickname 'Gator' (short for Navigator), and based at Mather Air Force Base (AFB) in California.

The variant is notable for having fewer windows along the fuselage, along with an array of external aerials to facilitate the equipment that could be found in the cabin. This was used to train pilots in various navigation systems and disciplines.

Later, some examples were converted to executive transports, with one (73-1149) lost in this role on a flight over Croatia in 1996 supporting United States European Command.

The T-43 fleet was retired on 17 September 2010 following a final mission out of Randolph AFB. One heavily modified NT-43A aircraft (73-1155) is still thought to be active, however. Based at secretive bases, it is rarely seen and sports unusual radomes on its nose and tail sections.

The military variant of the Boeing 737.

Chapter 4

European Operators

Europe was where the 737's commercial life began, and so it is a natural place to start this world tour of the carriers that flew the aircraft. Lufthansa took delivery of its first 737-130 in December 1967, with the first commercial flights beginning early in 1968. Thanks to the hype and attention it received, the aircraft was immediately popular and successful. Operating on domestic and European services from the airline's Frankfurt hub, the new Boeing was seen at many airports. (Aero Icarus)

With the 737-200 variant already in development before the -100 entered service, the United Kingdom's Britannia Airways became the first to order the type in Europe. A growing market for inclusive tour holiday travel was proving cut-throat, and so Britannia gambled that passengers would choose them if it offered modern, fast jet aircraft. The alternatives were the older propliners still used by the competition (and even Britannia until that point), which were slow and noisy.

Britannia was the first British airline to order the Boeing 737. Like the Bristol Britannia aircraft it replaced, the large fleet of 737-200s would become synonymous with the leisure airline. The first 737-200 to be delivered to Britannia was G-AVRL on 8 July 1968, making it the first airline in Europe to operate the -200 variant.

Above: Britannia Airways' long history with the Boeing 737-200 saw its fleet wear several different colour schemes. This was the second livery, seen on G-BADP. It would be slightly modified to replace the airline name with the simpler 'Britannia' in a large red font a few years later.

Right: Between 1968 and the mid-1990s, Britannia Airways' extensive fleet of Boeing 737-200 aircraft could be seen flying holidaymakers to destinations across Europe from airports all over the UK.

Seen only a year before it moved on to become a workhorse for Ryanair, Britannia 737-204 G-BTZF is seen at East Midlands airport in 1993 in the final livery worn. By this point, Britannia was already looking at replacement types such as the Boeing 757, but its 737-200s had served it well and proved to be a shrewd purchase. This aircraft would eventually be retired by Ryanair in 2004.

In 1974, British European Airways (BEA) and the British Overseas Airways Corporation (BOAC) were merged to form British Airways (BA) as the single national carrier. From that date it operated both short- and long-haul routes under one banner. With this merger came the decision to upgrade the fleet of aircraft, with a decision 'in principle' to order the Boeing 737-200. Slots were secured on the now very busy Boeing production line. The Department of Trade (which at the time was the airline's owner) relented on its 'Buy British' rule for the airline, which was seen by many – not least the airline's management – to be restricting its ability to grow and become profitable. Finally, it allowed the airline to order 19 of the American aircraft in July 1978.

Luxair, the national carrier of Luxembourg, took delivery of its first 737-200 in December 1977. It would operate four of the type before newer models took over in the early 1990s. For an airline with a mix of business and leisure routes over both short and medium-length journeys, the 737 made perfect sense as a capable all-rounder.

Ultimately, BA would operate 50 737-200s between 1977 and 2001, when newer Airbus A319s took over European and domestic schedules. Two of its aircraft are seen here at Birmingham two years apart, in 1997 and 1999, sporting the airline's so-called Landor livery (above), and then the Project Utopia 'World Images' Waves and Cranes livery depicting Japanese culture on the tail fin (below).

Transavia Holland was a new airline, founded in the late 1960s, to cater for the charter and leisure markets. Quick to realise the potential of the jet age, it ordered Sud Aviation Caravelles from 1969. The Boeing 737 was introduced by Transavia Holland to replace these Caravelles in 1974 and began a long association with the type, which still continues today. Keen to keep income flowing during quieter months, its aircraft were regularly seen on loan to other airlines.

An Air Belgium 737-200 is seen at Athens Hellinikon airport in 1982. This airline began operations as Abelag Airways in 1979, with a single 707 and 737-200. The name was changed in 1980. Its aircraft were used on leisure services from Brussels to destinations across Europe. (Bill Robertson)

Germany's Hapag Lloyd Flug was one of the many charter airlines founded by shipping companies during the growth of the leisure travel industry in the 1960s and '70s. Acquiring Boeing 727s to fly its cruise passengers, it quickly expanded to offer standalone flights and vacation packages to European destinations. The airline received the first of six 737-200s in June 1981 to supplement its 727 fleet. It would go on to become the launch customer for the 737-800 Next Generation model in 1998 and is today part of the giant TUI Group.

Air Europe was a new leisure airline founded in 1978 by industry veterans. Its focus was on taking a slice of the growing demand for inclusive tour and holiday flights to Europe from the United Kingdom. To set itself apart from the existing operators at the time, it began life with a fleet of three brand new Boeing 737-200 Advanced aircraft. Compared to the ageing fleets of competitors such as Dan-Air London, and even older model 737s at Britannia Airways, these gave Air Europe an edge. The aircraft were also more economical to run than older aircraft.

Following a successful start at London Gatwick, thanks in no small part to its team of industry veterans at the helm, Air Europe opened its second base in 1979 at Manchester Airport, UK, a year after its start. Boeing 737-2S3 G-BMSM is seen at that airport only a few months after delivery in 1980, ready to ferry 130 holidaymakers to the sun.

Aer Lingus was another early European adopter of the 737. Its fleet at the time included long-range Boeing 707s and 720s, and the BAC One-Eleven and Vickers Viscount on its European and UK services. With growing demand on some of its trunk routes, including Dublin to London, the 737-200 was ordered.

This classic 1970s view features one of these 737-200s. In total, some 17 different examples were operated by Aer Lingus at various times between 1969 and 1997.

EI-ASA was the first aircraft to arrive, in 1969, and is seen here still going strong 20 years later. The aircraft ended its career flying for the Peruvian Air Force. Later, Aer Lingus would fly the 737-300, -400 and -500. (John Kimberley)

Orion Airways, another British leisure airline, was based at East Midlands airport. It had a familiar livery of browns and oranges, which could be seen all over Europe at Mediterranean and winter resorts. It had additional bases at London Gatwick, Manchester and Birmingham and operated from most UK regional airports on charter work.

Orion Airways flew its Boeing 737-200s to destinations across Europe from bases in the UK. The airline merged with Britannia Airways in January 1989, but not before acquiring a fleet of 12 Boeing 737-200s (including the 737th Boeing 737), 737-300s and Airbus A300s.

This aircraft, a 737-2M8 registered G-BHCL, was leased to Orion Airways from Trans European Airways in 1980 for a year, yet it wore the airline's full livery. The aircraft later went on to fly for America West Airlines, WestJet in Canada, and Batavia Air in Indonesia. It was last seen being used as a restaurant to the west of the city of Surakarta on the island of Java.

Many holidaymakers will remember taking a Spantax flight on their holiday to the sun during the 1970s and '80s. The airline was founded in 1959 and went on to help establish the booming tourism industry in Spain. This Boeing 737-229 was leased from Sabena in 1987 and wears the airline's final livery before its demise in 1988.

Time Air Sweden, also known simply as Air Sweden, was a short-lived airline based at Stockholm operating scheduled services. One of three 737-200s it operated (alongside 737-300s, Lockheed L-1011 and Douglas DC-8s) is seen here at Frankfurt.

Belgian national carrier Sabena chose three 737-200C Combi variants as part of its original order for the type in the 1970s. Two more were added later. This 1990s livery displays the affiliation Sabena had with Swissair. Both airlines would disappear in the early 2000s following the downturn in the aviation industry after the September 2001 terrorist attacks in the United States.

Boeing 737-2K9 G-DFUB was one of six of the type operated by Monarch Airlines between 1981 and 1987 on leisure routes out of British airports. It is seen here on a winter charter flight at Geneva. Monarch had a mixed fleet, ranging from older Bristol Britannia propliners to BAC One-Elevens and Boeing 720s. Like Britannia with the 737, Monarch would become the first leisure airline to fly the brand-new Boeing 757 in 1983.

It was common for UK airlines such as Monarch to lease additional aircraft during busier summer months and lease their own aircraft out during the quieter winter. This Boeing 737-200, G-DWHH, was delivered to the airline in 1982, but as this hybrid livery shows it had recently been on lease to Pacific Western Airlines in Canada.

Maersk Air of Denmark had a strong association with the 737-200. It acquired its first examples in 1976, and went on to operate more than 20 of the type through the 1980s and early 1990s. These were assigned duties flying domestic and regional flights, charter services to the sun, and many went on lease to other carriers to supplement Maersk's income during quieter months. The airline went on to operate the 737-300, -400, -500 and -700 until it eventually closed in 2005.

The Boeing 737-200 proved very popular at Air Malta, the national carrier of the tiny Mediterranean island popular with holidaymakers. It operated nine different examples between 1983 and 2004, including some leased from other carriers. This example is on loan from Transavia in the Netherlands.

Dan-Air London followed Britannia Airways in introducing the Boeing 737-200 on its leisure and scheduled services from the UK. Its management felt that introducing the Advanced version of the 737-200 would help it leapfrog rival Britannia (which still operated many early-build 737s) in the charter market, as it offered better field performance and was cheaper to run.

With the arrival of the 737-200 into its fleet, Dan-Air introduced its new corporate livery. However, the first aircraft to arrive wore the older livery. In this picture, two of the airline's 737s can be seen wearing the carrier's different liveries; G-BKAP in the background has the older scheme, whilst G-BLDE in the foreground wears the newer scheme. The author remembers many flights on these aircraft to holiday destinations in the 1980s.

A Britannia Airways Boeing 737-200 in a hybrid livery, on loan from Aer Lingus in the summer of 1987. Leisure airlines, like Britannia, sought to provide a year-round programme of holiday flights, but naturally the summer was the busier time and could be supported by leasing additional aircraft.

BA felt the pressure of the growing leisure market and operated its own charter division known as British Airtours. Traditionally provided with aircraft from the mainline fleet, it operated the 737-200 from 1982. Nine of these aircraft were transferred from BA to operate holiday routes to the sun, in a similar livery to its parent, from bases at London Gatwick and Manchester. Popular destinations in France, Greece, Portugal and Spain were served.

KLM briefly supplemented its Boeing 737-300 and Douglas DC-9 fleets with three leased 737-200s on and off between 1988 and 1995. All were leased from Transavia Airlines, part-owned by KLM since 1991. Here, PH-TVX wears the full livery of the national carrier and is seen in 1988.

PH-TVR, also owned by Transavia but leased to KLM, is seen at Amsterdam Schiphol airport in the late 1980s.

Lufthansa's order for the 737-100 allowed Boeing to officially launch the aircraft. However, the move fell victim to its own success and Lufthansa found the aircraft too small for its needs, much as United Airlines had predicted. It, therefore, followed up with an order for -200 models in 1969, which would supplement and then replace the smaller -100s. The first delivery, a 737-200C combination passenger and cargo variant, arrived later that year. In total, 47 -200s were flown by Lufthansa before the type was retired in 1998.

Lufthansa's D-ABHF seen in 1983. The airline's aircraft were used on a busy network of scheduled services across Europe from its main hubs in Germany.

Spanish leisure airline Hispania was a familiar sight across the United Kingdom and other European airports throughout the 1980s. It started charter services with Sud Aviation Caravelles, before adding three Boeing 737-200s in 1985. This example, EC-DVN, was leased from Transavia Airlines from 1985 until 1988, shortly before the airline ceased flying due to financial difficulties.

Airways International Cymru was the airline arm of Red Dragon Travel, based at Cardiff in Wales. Having started life with a BAC One-Eleven, it flew this former Britannia Airways 737-204 from 1985, and added a 737-300 the following year. The airline ceased flying in 1988.

Immediately following the demise of Airways International Cymru, a new carrier known as Amberair launched with two 737s. BOSA, previously G-BASI, and is seen at a rainy Manchester in July 1988 preparing for a flight to Malaga.

Air France was relatively late in joining the 737 club. Its first example arrived in 1982 from an order for 17 examples, mostly leased rather than bought outright. At the time, the airline was already operating the 727-200 on European services. However, its large fleet of French-built Sud Aviation Caravelles was being replaced, and a new type was needed to fly the domestic and short-haul routes it had served well for over 20 years.

The 737-200s were followed up with orders for the -300 and -500 models in the late 1980s. However, the introduction of the Airbus A320 family of airlines in 1987 soon became the focus of Air France's fleet for decades to come, and the 737-200s were all gone by 2002.

Closer inspection of this Air France Boeing 737-200 will reveal an unusual registration. Instead of the usual F- prefix denoting French ownership, it actually has the American registration N-4504F. At the time of this shot, this aircraft was being leased by Air France from a US company to operate regional flights out of Pointe-à-Pitre in Guadeloupe.

Following the merger between British Airways and British Caledonian in April 1988, the national airline chose to rebrand its British Airtours subsidiary as Caledonian. The new branding sought to keep the memories of British Caledonian alive, with some similarities in its aircraft livery. Otherwise, operations were similar to that of British Airtours, operating leisure services to the sun, and utilising a mixed fleet of mostly former BA aircraft. These included the Boeing 737-200, 747-200, 757-200, Lockheed TriStar and Airbus A320 over its history, including this aircraft, which was leased for six months in 1989.

This 1977-built 737-204 Advanced was briefly preserved at the Museo Nacional de Aeronáutica de Argentina in Buenos Aires following retirement by Aerolineas Argentinas as LV-YZA. In this picture, it is shown earning its keep for Britannia Airways as G-BECH on another holiday charter. It was eventually scrapped in 2013.

TAP Air Portugal had entered the jet age in 1962 with the Sud Aviation Caravelle, but soon became a customer of Boeing products when it introduced the 707 and 727 to its fleet in 1965 and 1967, respectively. Relatively late to add the 737-200, its first example joined the fleet in 1983 and the type remained with the airline until 1999. The 737-300 was also a part of the airline's fleet until a move to Airbus products in the 1990s.

Air Atlantis was set up in 1985 by TAP Air Portugal to operate charter flights from destinations across Europe bringing holidaymakers into Portugal's resorts. It used TAP's aircraft on its flights, which wore this livery reminiscent of the parent airline.

Part of Lufthansa's large 1969 order for Boeing 737-200s, D-ABFT was allocated to partner airline Condor, which flew leisure services from Germany's airports to holiday destinations. The aircraft did, however, fly on lease to Lufthansa briefly in 1988 before being sold to TAP Air Portugal. (Ralph Pfeiffer)

Olympic Airways was one of Europe's most diverse and interesting airlines, owned and managed for many years by Greek shipping magnate Aristotle Onassis. Shortly after his death in 1975, the airline was returned to state ownership and an order for 11 Boeing 737-200s was placed, supplementing the extant fleet of Boeing 707s, 720s, 727s and various other short-haul types.

The 737 would become a workhorse of the airline, flying domestic, regional and Europe-wide services. Here, SX-BCD, the fourth to arrive, is seen in 1995. Later, Olympic would add the 737-300 and -400 variants. However, the airline would eventually succumb to generations of poor financial management and close in 2009.

At the opening of the 1990s, the newly independent country of Croatia needed its own national carrier. Croatia Airlines started services in 1991 with a McDonnell Douglas MD-82. Three Boeing 737-200s were leased from Lufthansa in 1992, including this one, which was seen on services all over Europe.

During the late 1990s, BA chose to base aircraft at its regional bases in Birmingham and Manchester. It advertised this fact by applying titles on the upper fuselages of some of its fleet – in particular the 737-200s that were based at these outposts. This example is G-BGDE, taxiing out at Birmingham but wearing the Manchester title. The distinctions were soon lost with the retraction of most routes away from the regions back into the airline's London Gatwick and Heathrow hubs.

Luxair's LX-LGH is seen at Palma de Mallorca in Spain, supplementing the airline's scheduled services with summer charter flying.

Giving away its true ownership, the registration of this Lithuanian Airlines aircraft is LY-GPA. It was leased to the airline from the GPA Group in 1992 as the newly independent country's national airline sought to establish a route network out of the capital city Vilnius. Interestingly, the aircraft had been sub-leased to the airline in 1991 from MALÉV, which was operating it temporarily. (Robbie Shaw)

OO-TEL of Trans European Airways (TEA) at Birmingham in 1989. TEA had been founded in 1970 by the TIFA tour operator to capitalise on the holiday market, much the same as was seen in other Northern European countries at the time. It introduced Boeing 707s and 720s and was the only operator of the Airbus A300B1 model. The first 737 arrived in 1976.

Inter European Airways leased this former Maersk 737-2L9 in May 1987 to launch flights from Cardiff that summer. It was returned to the lessor the following year, and replaced by two 737-300s. This charter airline arm of Aspro Travel was acquired by Airtours in 1993.

Atlantic Island Air of Iceland owned this 737, TF-AIC, which formerly flew with Braathens SAFE. It is seen here with Atlantsflug titles in 1992. (Schneider Herwart)

Ambassador Airways was a start-up airline that flew holiday charters to mostly Greek destinations from UK regional airports between 1992–1994. Its fleet included two former Britannia 737-200s.

Still wearing its British registration following 13 years flying for British Airways, this 737-236 is seen at London Gatwick in the livery of Russian carrier Transaero Airlines. It would later take on the registration RA-73002, eventually being scrapped at Moscow in 2007.

Beginning as a regional airline, Ryanair transformed into a point-to-point low-cost carrier in the early 1990s, and took on a fleet of second-hand Boeing 737-200s previously flown by airlines such as Britannia Airways. These were available at bargain prices and would enable the airline to establish a wide network of routes attracting passengers with its offering of cheap fares. In all, some 20 -200s were operated, and surprisingly many went on to operate for other airlines following replacement, despite high utilisation by Ryanair.

Ryanair operated 21 Boeing 737-200s between 1994 and 2007, largely sourced from the former Britannia Airways fleet, as well as Lufthansa. The Irish airline went on to acquire newer 737-800 Next Generation aircraft from the mid-2000s.

A number of Ryanair's 737-200 fleet wore non-standard liveries. These included billboard schemes advertising different brands. This example, however, wore a large airline title on an otherwise white fuselage.

Ryanair 737-204 Advanced EI-CJE in the special Eircell 'Ready to Go' livery. A number of Ryanair's aircraft wore advertising like this. Once retired, this aircraft could be seen for many years being used as a training aid for the fire service at Dublin Airport, still in its blue and purple scheme.

Above: Sabre Airways was established in 1994 to operate charter services on behalf of tour operators. It began life with two former Britannia Airways 737-204s, and soon added two former Dan-Air London 727-200s. The airline later rebranded as XL Airways. (Robbie Shaw)

Left: From 1971, Britannia Airways' Boeing 737s typically flew with the maximum 130-seat capacity. However, some of its fleet, including this example, were combi variants that could be converted to carry cargo. This allowed the airline to make extra revenue during quiet periods, carrying cargoes as varied as racehorses and newspapers.

The Boeing 737-200 was the first Western-built jet aircraft to be ordered by MALÉV as Hungary approached the end of the era of Soviet influence in 1989. It would operate six of the type, as well as the 737-300, -400 and -500, and 737-600, -700 and -800 Next Generation models. Sadly, MALÉV ceased trading in 2012.

While carriers including Southwest Airlines in the United States had pioneered the low-cost, so-called 'no frills' airline model in the 1970s, the boom in low-cost carriers did not begin to gather pace until the late 1990s. easyJet in the United Kingdom was an early adopter of the model and has grown to become one of Europe's largest carriers today, with more than 300 aircraft.

Back in 1995, easyJet started flying with a pair of leased Boeing 737-200s linking London Luton with both Edinburgh and Glasgow. In its early days, the airline's telephone number was emblazoned along the fuselage, before the website address replaced it a few years later. It shows how far the model of online booking has come.

easyJet would go on to operate a fleet of Boeing 737-300s and later -700 Next Generation variants, before moving on to Airbus types.

Charter airline Lauda Air was formed by Formula One racing legend Niki Lauda in 1979 using BAC One-Eleven aircraft. In 1985, a fleet of Boeing 737s were added, including this -200 model leased from Transavia Holland. Later, 737-300 and -400 models were also flown, along with Next Generation variants in the 1990s. The airline was merged into Austrian Airlines in 2013, but the Lauda name lives on as a new airline under the Ryanair banner today.

Lufthansa 737-230 D-ABHE began life carrying passengers as part of the follow-up order the airline placed to replace the original batch of 737-100s. In 1985, it was decided to convert this aircraft and a few others to freighters, which would join the new Lufthansa Cargo division (and briefly the subsidiary airline German Cargo). It would fly in this role until 1999 when it was leased, and then sold, to Air Atlanta Iceland.

Fly Europa was a short-lived airline launched in the UK in 2000. It had an affiliation with Spain's Air Europa, as evident from the livery worn by G-CEAF, a 737-229 leased from European Air Charter. Sadly, the venture did not last.

Right: F-GCLL is seen at Paris flying for French leisure carrier Euralair. This particular aircraft is one of the early batches of 737s ordered by United Airlines and was the 63rd aircraft off the production line. It first flew in August 1968. The fact the aircraft carried on flying until 2003 demonstrates the longevity of these airframes. (Bill Robertson)

Below: Trans European Airways Boeing 737-2M8 OO-TEN taxis to the gate at Luton airport, shortly before being sold to America West Airlines as N141AW. Whilst TEA was a Belgian airline, it had divisions in the UK, France, Italy and Switzerland.

Chapter 5
North American Operators

United Airlines was the first to commit to the Boeing 737 in North America. It came as a great relief to Boeing, which had been looking for custom with one of the big carriers against competition from Douglas and other manufacturers in its home market.

The deal was secured when Boeing agreed to enlarge the original 737-100 to become the -200 model, with greater seating capacity. United ordered 40, and development of the variant ran alongside the -100 model.

A very early Boeing 737-200, N9015U, was the 34th built. It flew with United Airlines its entire life, from delivery in 1968 until retirement in 1998, carrying millions of passengers safely in the process.

Western Airlines was one of the few US carriers to adopt the 737 in the early days. The Californian carrier already had the Boeing 707 and 727 in its fleet, but was looking to replace its older Lockheed L-188 Electra turboprop aircraft on shorter and thinner routes. Adding the 737-200 allowed it to become an all-jet carrier. (Bill Robertson)

Western began life in 1926 and grew to become one of California's largest carriers, with a widespread reach across the United States, Canada and other destinations. Following its merger with Delta Air Lines in September 1986, much of the fleet continued to fly in a hybrid livery until opportunities to repaint were found. This 1969-built 737-200, N4521W, would be sold to Braniff in 1988.

Piedmont entered the jet age with the Boeing 727 in 1967 and, like Western, was quick to follow up with the 737-200 in 1968 as one of the first operators in America. It would become one of the largest operators of the type in the world, with 63 examples passing through the airline's fleet. The majority joined in the late 1980s as the airline was expanding rapidly. Piedmont would soon be merged into USAir, where these aircraft would go on to provide many more years of service.

N743N is an early build 737-201 delivered to Piedmont Airlines in 1969. It would carry on flying with USAir as N212US following the airlines' merger in 1989.

Air California was a pioneer of low-cost air travel launched in Orange County in 1967 and offering intrastate services. Airline deregulation in 1978 allowed it to expand its horizons to other states.

Another of the early American adopters of the 737, the airline had acquired its first -200 on lease in 1969. The capabilities of the new aircraft were described as 'highly compatible' with Orange County Airport, allowing steeper departures to satisfy noise abatement procedures. Air California later acquired the two former Avianca Colombia 737-100s in 1977 and 1979, respectively. The airline later rebranded as AirCal, and these vintage jets briefly went on to fly for American Airlines following the two airlines' merger in 1987.

One of the many 737s flown by the original Frontier Airlines, based at Denver Stapleton Airport, until it ceased flying in 1986. For a while, the airline's entire jet fleet was made up of 737-200s, following the retirement of its 727s, and before the introduction of the McDonnell Douglas MD-80 series in 1982.

Whilst it wasn't the first airline to operate on a low-cost model, Southwest's focus on utilising a single aircraft fleet to reduce training and maintenance costs, while developing an aggressive point-to-point network, was pioneering.

The 737 was a great fit for Southwest, which had briefly trialled using 727s. It offered the right costs and good dispatch reliability and was self-sufficient enough to not require jet bridges or air stairs, meaning turnarounds could be much quicker. Its aircraft had 112 seats.

Flying initially within Texas on routes from Dallas to Houston and San Antonio, and representing its desert background using bold orange, red and gold colours, when the Airline Deregulation Act came in 1978, Southwest was able to vastly increase its presence across the United States. As a result, its fleet of 737-200s grew too.

N61SW was delivered as part of Southwest Airlines' expansion post-deregulation. It allowed the airline to expand into new markets outside Texas for the first time, helping it grow to become the giant low-cost carrier that it has now become.

Today, Southwest is one of America's largest carriers and is the world's largest 737 operator with close to 800 aircraft in its fleet. It was the launch customer for the 737-300, -500, -700 and the upcoming 737 MAX 7. Its 737-200s were finally withdrawn in 2005. (Bill Robertson)

Pan American (Pan Am) was not particularly known for operating the 737. More recognised for its 707 and 727 fleets, its lack of a domestic network meant it had little need for a short-haul airliner. However, from 1950 until 1990, the airline was heavily involved in the Internal German Services network, linking Berlin with cities in West Germany, which had come about following the end of World War Two. In fact, for many years Pan Am was the largest airline at Berlin Tempelhof airport by passenger numbers handled. From 1982, Pan Am acquired 16 737-200s, all second-hand, mostly to service these German routes.

N70723 was leased to Pan Am from Aloha Airlines from 1983 to 1988 and is seen here arriving at Frankfurt from Berlin.

Air Florida began flying in 1971 and grew as a major leisure airline linking destinations around the United States with those in Florida. Its fleet comprised a variety of aircraft, including both 737-200s, and six ageing -100s, including N48AF seen here. Having joined the airline in August 1980 following service with Malaysia-Singapore Airlines and its successor Singapore Airlines, this aircraft would go on to fly with the Mexican Air Force from 1981.

As a long-time customer of Douglas aircraft, Delta Air Lines naturally chose this manufacturer for its jet aircraft in the late 1950s. It was not until the early 1970s that the first Boeing aircraft were ordered, with the 727 and 747. The first of 75 Boeing 737-200s were acquired from 1983, with this example, N325DL, arriving a year later. It is seen here at Miami International Airport in 1994. The fleet was bolstered by the merger with Western in 1989.

By the time America West Airlines was founded in 1981, the Boeing 737-200 had already been in service for nearly 15 years and many US carriers were looking at the newer generation 737 models for fleet growth. This meant older -100s and -200s were available at good prices to help the start-up airline get off the ground. The example here, N138AW, was relatively young, having rolled off the production line in 1982 and joining the airline in 1984. (David J Hamilton)

America West Airlines leased this 737-275 from Canadian Airlines for almost ten years, during which time it retained its non-US registration of C-GCPW. It is seen here at the airline's home base Phoenix Sky Harbor in 1995. (Robbie Shaw)

Casino Express was an airline set up to ferry gamblers and vacationers to Elko, Nevada, from 1989. Seven 737-200s were acquired for this purpose, including this former PSA and Air New Zealand example, N457TM seen at Detroit in 1995.

Through many different guises and business models, this company is still alive today operating as the low-cost carrier Avelo Airlines with Next Generation 737s. (Robbie Shaw)

The original Braniff International Airways, a once-proud US carrier known for its bright colour schemes and wide-ranging network across North, Central and South America, Asia and Europe, ceased operations in 1982 and never operated any variant of the Boeing 737.

Following its demise, some of the airline's assets were acquired and a new carrier founded in 1984 under the name Braniff Inc. It initially flew Boeing 727-200s, and leased ten 737-200s, including this example. It, too, would suffer bankruptcy in 1989, the year this picture was taken. A third incarnation of Braniff would emerge between 1991 and 92, with a similar fate. This particular aircraft crashed in 1991 whilst operating for Faucett Perú.

Bahamasair operated a total of 17 Boeing 737-200s at various times. Here are three examples of its aircraft in action.

In this first picture, C6-BDZ approaches Nassau. This aircraft was leased from Belgium's Trans European Airways for six months at the start of 1979, and wears a hybrid livery.

Air Belgium sub-leased this Boeing 737-247 to Bahamasair in 1980. It is seen at Miami in March of that year.

One of the most attractive and colourful liveries to have adorned the 737-200 is that worn by Bahamasair during the 1980s, with its gold and blue representing the sand and sea of the idyllic islands off the Florida coast.

Magnicharters leased this early 737-247 in 1994 to use on leisure and domestic services in Mexico. The aircraft began life in 1969 with Western Airlines, before going on to see service with many other carriers around the world. It was finally retired in Peru in 2004.

This airframe started life as one of the batches of 737s ordered by Britannia Airways in the early 1970s. It joined the fleet as G-BAZI in 1974 before being sold on in 1985. It remained a familiar sight in the UK flying for Airways International Cymru, Amberair and Paramount Airlines, acquiring the registration G-BOSA in 1988 (and already seen in the previous chapter).

Servicios Aerolineas Mexicanas (SAM) leased the aircraft in 1994, and it is seen here still wearing its UK registration. It later became XA-STE. In 1996, it was acquired by Skyjet, with stints leased to National Airlines and Avant Airlines, before being sold to LAN Airlines as CC-CSP in 2001. Finally broken up in 2006, the cockpit went on to become a learning aid at the LAN Training School in Santiago de Chile.

Arriving relatively late to the fleet of Cayman Airways, VP-CAL started its life with Braathens S.A.F.E. in Norway. It joined the Caribbean airline in 1995. The airline had, however, leased its first 737-200 in 1986 and operated a total of nine examples until 2008. Today, the airline maintains a 737 service with a fleet of four MAX examples.

Moving north into Canada, Quebecair acquired this Boeing 737-296 from the manufacturer in 1980 as C-GQBB. It went on lease to Pan Am for two years from 1983 and used the registration N387PA, before returning to its owner. It is seen here before the Canadian registration was re-applied. Once a proud name in Canadian aviation with a widespread domestic network, Quebecair was merged with CP Air and Pacific Western Airlines in 1986 to create Canadian Airlines, with whom this aircraft continued flying for another 15 years. (Gary Vincent)

WestJet is a shining example of how the Boeing 737-200 still had a useful role to bring to the aviation industry's latest ventures some 30 years after it first flew. The airline was founded to offer low-cost competition to Canada's established carriers and began flying in 1996, linking the country's principal cities.

The airline's initial fleet comprised two veteran aircraft built in the early 1970s, which had already flown for a number of carriers. Undoubtedly cheap to acquire, they provided the perfect launch model for this new carrier, which became an affordable alternative to full-service airlines. Soon WestJet would acquire more -200s as its network grew, with 25 examples in service at its peak. The final 737-200 service was flown by WestJet in 2005, at which time more modern 737 Next Generation models had been added. Today, MAX variants are being added to the fleet.

A number of former WestJet 737-200s are preserved at technical training colleges in Canada and the UK.

Following the merger of Canadian Airlines and Air Canada in 2001, the national carrier enjoyed something of a monopoly on air travel in the country. That is until upstart low-cost carriers such as WestJet (see previous picture) started to challenge the high fares, and Air Canada was forced to respond. It did so by starting its own low-cost brands, including Tango and Zip Air.

This Boeing 737-217 Advanced had been delivered to CP Air in 1981, becoming Canadian Airlines in 1987. It became part of Air Canada following their merger, and later flew in both the Zip Air and Tango schemes during 2002–03, shortly before the venture was cancelled. The aircraft enjoyed a few more years flying for Merpati in Indonesia before being retired.

Frontier Airlines was a well-known face of American aviation from the 1950s until 1986, and a user of the Boeing 737-200. So, when some former employees decided to resurrect the name with a new airline in 1994, they chose the -200 as their start-up type owing to its familiarity and affordability on the second-hand market.

Still flying today, albeit with modern Airbus aircraft, the airline still applies images of wildlife to each side of its aircraft tail. This example, N270FL, sported a snowy owl on the starboard side.

Above: It was not uncommon for start-up and charter carriers in the 1990s and 2000s to take on Boeing 737-200s, which were being retired en masse by many of the world's mainline carriers. WinAir was one such airline. Based at Long Beach, California, it acquired five 737-200s including this ex-British Airways example in 1998 to operate sports charters, and later tried offering low-cost passenger charter services to various destinations. Sadly, the airline closed the following year after running into financial difficulties. (David J Hamilton)

Below: Another example of WinAir's Boeing 737 fleet, N118RW is seen at Tucson, Arizona, in 1998.

This picture shows an example of the common practice of Boeing 737s spending periods on loan to other airlines outside of peak travel times for their owners. EI-ASH was a 737-248 owned by Aer Lingus and spent many winters between 1973 and 1987 on such leases, when demand was low in Europe but higher elsewhere – particularly in North America. Here, the colours of California's AirCal adorn the aircraft in 1985, and only the registration gives away its true ownership. Many European airlines would lease extra aircraft capacity during the busy summer months.

March 2008 saw the final scheduled services by the Boeing 737-200 within the United States. Hawaiian intra-island operator Aloha Airlines had taken its first examples, known as 'Funbirds', in 1969 and enjoyed a long history with the type, with some 13 examples operated over the next 39 years.

   They were put to good use, flying many daily departures between the different islands in the Pacific chain. In 1988, one of Aloha's 737s suffered the partial loss of its cabin roof during a flight, with the crew performing a miraculous landing. The explosive decompression was put down to metal fatigue, owing to years of flying in the humid, salty air of Hawaii.

Chapter 6
South and Central American Operators

Brazilian carrier VARIG operated a wide-ranging fleet of aircraft over the years, with early jet airliners including the Caravelle joining in 1959, and the Boeing 707 and 727 from 1960 and 1970, respectively. While many piston and turboprop types were active through the 1980s and '90s, the airline settled on a large fleet of Boeing 737-200s, which were acquired from 1974 and became the mainstay of the domestic and regional trunk routes until retired in 2003.

Copa Airlines acquired its first jet aircraft, a Boeing 737-100, in 1980. It would later add more than 20 737-200s, which served as the backbone of its network of routes out of Panama City from 1988 until 2005 when modern Next Generation 737 models took over.

Aerolineas Argentinas operated this 737-287 for its entire service life, between July 1970 and its eventual retirement and scrapping in 2000. The 737 arrived at the Argentinian carrier as part of an upgrade of its fleet, replacing older de Havilland Comets and Sud Aviation Caravelles with more modern types. The Boeing 727 and 747 would also be added during the 1970s.

The Boeing 737-200 had a long and successful history in Argentina, flying with many of the country's airlines. It was commonly used on domestic and regional sectors, and scenes like this at the Buenos Aires Aeroparque domestic airport were common, with aircraft coming and going on flights throughout the day.

TACA International (now flying as Avianca El Salvador) is one of Central America's oldest airlines, having been founded in 1931. Its first jet aircraft was the BAC One-Eleven, but it later chose the Boeing 737-200 as the focus of its regional fleet. Some 16 examples operated between 1982 and 2005. N861L, which was brand new at the time, is seen at Miami International in 1982. (Bill Robertson)

Above: Aviateca Guatemala had flown a wide variety of aircraft types, both propeller and jet driven, until its fleet focused on the Boeing 737 in 1990. It flew 12 of the 737-200 models, including N121GA pictured here, and nine -300s. These were replaced by the Airbus A320 family from 2006. The airline is now known as Avianca Guatemala. (Robbie Shaw)

Left: Many aircraft in Britannia's fleet went on to fly with carriers around the world when sold in the mid-1990s. This example is seen with National Airlines of Chile shortly after delivery, and still wearing the familiar Britannia blue pinstripes.

LV-LEB of Aerolineas Argentinas about to depart Buenos Aires Aeroparque in May 2004, a month before it was retired. This aircraft survives as a ground trainer at Hoofddorp in the Netherlands. (David J Hamilton)

Also spotted at Buenos Aires Aeroparque towards the end of the 737-200s service in South America is LV-ZYX of regional carrier Southern Winds. This is a former Royal Brunei, Air New Zealand and LAN Chile aircraft, which was 27 years old at the time.

Right and below: A former Sabena aircraft, here are two shots of YV-74C working for Servivensa of Venezuela. The aircraft joined the airline in 1996 for the final years of its life.

The two pictures here were both taken at Miami International in 1997 and 1999, respectively, and show two different liveries worn by the airline. The aircraft would be retired in 2002.

Avant Airlines leased this 737-229 in 1997 for three years, operating it on domestic sectors within Chile. The airline was known for the variety of colour combinations worn by its aircraft. It flew nine different -200s before closing down in 2001.

Costa Rica's LACSA was a relative latecomer to operating the 737, having already flown many other jet types since the 1960s. The first 737-200 arrived in 1992, and 11 examples would be flown – mostly on lease, such as this aircraft – at different times. The final one left in 2004 when modern Airbus types were added.

The Venezuelan Air Force was another military operator of the 737-200. Unlike the US Air Force, this operator did not use its aircraft for testing or airborne intelligence, but instead as a VIP transport not too dissimilar to standard airline models. 0207 flew in this role until 2019 and was still active with ConViasa flying passengers until recently.

Líneas Aéreas Privadas Argentinas, more commonly known as LAPA Airlines, was an Argentinian carrier founded in 1977. As well as a widespread domestic network, the airline flew to destinations across South America and to the United States prior to its bankruptcy in 2003.

Of its fleet of Boeing 737-200s, one was involved in a fatal accident in 1999 where the aircraft failed to become airborne on take-off and careered across a road and onto a golf course.

The aircraft in this shot, LV-WNA, went on to fly in Indonesia. The picture demonstrates how the position of the thrust reversers on the Boeing 737-200s JT8D engines would commonly cause exhaust marks along the rear fuselage of the aircraft, which frequently had to be cleaned.

Chapter 7
Asian and Australasian Operators

National Airways Corporation (NAC) was New Zealand's domestic airline prior to being amalgamated into Air New Zealand in 1978. It started life as part of the country's air force following World War Two, growing steadily during peacetime. The first jet aircraft to be ordered by the airline was the Boeing 737-200 – chosen because of its capabilities at challenging airports like Wellington, and because it would allow the airline to continue growing. The New Zealand government had wanted the airline to purchase BAC One-Elevens, but the Boeing jet was favoured on economics, and thus ordered in 1966. This aircraft, ZK-NAC, was the first to arrive two years later.

Malaysian Airline System (MAS) became an independent carrier in 1972, following its split from ties with Singapore, when it was known as Malaysia-Singapore Airlines. With the Singapore carrier retaining the 737-100 fleet, MAS acquired 25 new 737-200s to serve on its domestic network. Here, 9M-MBH rests between flights at the old Kuala Lumpur Subang airport in 1976.

Royal Brunei Airlines started life in 1974 when two Boeing 737-200s were acquired for services to destinations around South East Asia. This was one of those aircraft, seen at London Heathrow on delivery to the airline. In total, four of the type were operated, including a -200C variant.

All Nippon Airways (ANA) was one of the earliest customers of the Boeing 737 in Asia. With domestic travel in Japan growing fast, this airline was looking to modernise its smaller, slower turboprop fleets. The Boeing 737, aimed at shorter routes, was perfect to complement the airline's existing Boeing 727s. An order for 16 aircraft saw the first arrive in 1969, with a follow-up order for a further six examples in the late 1970s.

This aircraft, JA8405, wears a large '05' under the cockpit and was, unsurprisingly, the fifth example to join the fleet, in January 1970. Being an early 737 airframe, it was sold on in 1976, with newer Advanced models joining the fleet. ANA was the first airline to fly the 737-200 Advanced.

This image shows an airline in transition. Southwest Air Lines had been formed in 1967 as a domestic carrier in Japan. It took delivery of its first Boeing 737-200 in 1979 and through the 1980s would acquire eight more. The airline changed its name to Japan TransOcean Air in 1993, and this image shows the new title on JA8475, which is still wearing the old airline's livery.

In the early 1980s, the Civil Aviation Administration of China (CAAC) ordered ten Boeing 737-200s in a bid to modernise the fleet of aircraft in its national airline. These started arriving in 1983, and in 1988 this giant national organisation was split into six regional airlines. The fleet, including its 737s, were distributed among these carriers, with three going to Air China, including this example.

In 1989, a China Airlines Boeing 737-200 like this one crashed into a mountain near Hualian on a domestic flight. The airline operated seven of the type, including this example seen in 1991.

Above: Far Eastern Air Transport was a domestic and regional carrier based in Taiwan, which existed from 1957 until 2019. During that period, it chose the Boeing 737 as part of its varied fleet of turboprop and jet aircraft. It flew the -200 model, like B-2615 seen here in 1984, from 1976. Interestingly, it also acquired two of Lufthansa's 737-130 fleet in 1981, which remained with the airline until the mid-1990s.

Right: 9H-MBY was leased to Malaysian Airline System in 1981–82 from Maersk Air. (A V Petersen)

Lao Aviation was formed in 1979 when Royal Air Lao and Lao Air Lines merged. Today, it is known as Lao Airlines. It operated this 737-291 between 1993 and 1996, and is seen here still wearing the registration of its previous identity flying for Frontier Airlines in the USA. It would later become RDPL-34125.

Air Great Wall was one of the many smaller carriers to emerge from the break-up of the centrally operated CAAC in China in the early 1990s. It began services using two Tupolev Tu-154Ms, replaced by three Air China 737-200s in 1995. One is seen here around that time at Chongqing. The airline eventually became part of China Eastern Airlines, and this aircraft was sold to a Sudanese company.

Above: Many of the world's ageing 737-200s found their way to Indonesia in the late 1990s, where a raft of start-up carriers were clamouring for cheap aircraft to begin domestic services in this country of vast area and population. Kartika Airlines was one of these airlines, starting up in 2001 with three of these aircraft. It would cease flying in 2010.

Left: Airfast is one of the many Indonesian airlines to have operated the Boeing 737-200. Unlike many other carriers, it primarily serves the oil, mining and construction industries, and is still active today, albeit without its trusty 737s.

Asian and Australasian Operators

Bouraq Indonesia Airlines was one of Indonesia's older airlines and was operating before the wave of start-up companies emerged in the 1990s. The airline began with piston and turboprop airliners, and introduced the Boeing 737-200 in 1993. They flew with the airline for 12 years, until 2005.

ModiLuft was one of India's first private carriers set up following the deregulation of the airline industry in 1993. It was a joint venture between an Indian businessman and Germany's Lufthansa, which provided four Boeing 737-230s, along with pilots, maintenance and training. The airline flew regional services from Delhi's main airport. A breakdown in the business relationship led to the airline closing down in 1996.

Wearing the colours of short-lived Pacific Transair of Australia, this Boeing 737-291 was on lease to Air Philippines, as the titles suggest. A regional carrier based at Subic Bay, Air Philippines grew to operate a fleet of almost 30 737-200s between 1996 and 2009. This example flew with the airline for only five months in late 1996.

Air Philippines today is known as PAL Express and flies as a partner of national carrier Philippine Airlines. Its fleet of 737-200s flew until 2009.

The domestic arm of Thai Airways acquired three 737-200s from 1977. Two of this fleet would crash in the mid-1980s, leaving aircraft, HS-TBA, as the lone 737. Therefore, a further two examples were acquired as replacements, before the domestic and international parts of the airline were merged in 1988. This picture is taken shortly after the merger, when the new livery was applied.

Air India did not fly the 737-200, despite its popularity with other carriers in the region. In fact, the five aircraft it eventually acquired only arrived in 2007 following its merger with Indian Airlines. These aircraft, including VT-EGM pictured here, were retained for use as freighters until retirement in 2011. (Sean DSilva)

Chapter 8
African and Middle East Operators

DETA (Direcção de Exploração de Transportes Aéreos) was Mozambique's government-run national airline between 1936 and 1980, when it was renamed LAM Linhas Aéreas de Moçambique. This aircraft flew with the airline all its life, from delivery in 1969, until it was damaged beyond repair in a landing accident in 1983.

South Africa has seen many different airlines operate the 737-200. Chief among them is national carrier South African Airways, which introduced the type in 1968, replacing its older Vickers Viscounts in the 1970s and Boeing 727-100s in the early 1980s. Including two freighter variants, some 31 examples were flown by the airline until they were retired in 2013. ZS-SIJ, pictured here, joined the fleet in 1982 and was transferred to subsidiary Safair in 2000, before being sold in South America in 2006.

Royal Air Maroc, the national carrier of Morocco, had been an early adopter of jet aircraft when it ordered the Sud Aviation Caravelle in 1958. It would also add the Boeing 727 in 1970. In 1975, the airline decided to replace its Caravelles with three Boeing 737-200s. The fleet would grow, with a fourth example added in 1981 and a Combi example joining in 1982. This aircraft, CN-RMJ, was one of the original batch and was retired by the airline in 2001.

Left: A Zambia Airways 737-2M9 Advanced with registration 9J-AEG. Unlike many African carriers, this airline acquired the aircraft from new in 1976, selling it to VASP in Brazil in 1995.

Below: Air Tanzania was a brand-new airline formed out of the ashes of East African Airways in 1977. Thanks to strong financial backing, it was able to acquire two Boeing 737-200s, alongside leased Fokker F27s and DHC-6 Twin Otters. This example, 5H-MRK, flew with the airline for 20 years until being sold in 1999 and going on to fly for a variety of carriers in South Africa. It is still active today, flying for Glencore Canada supporting mining operations.

This Boeing 737-2F9 Advanced spent its whole life flying for the once-proud Nigeria Airways. It was delivered in 1983 and has remained stored at Lagos International airport since the airline's demise in 2003, though it was used for a spell as a ground trainer for the airport fire services. It was one of 25 operated by the airline on its African services.

The government of Niger Republic ordered this Boeing 737-200 as a VIP transport aircraft from new in 1978. The prestige of a new Boeing aircraft, combined with its capabilities for flying in the developing world made it a good choice for this customer. This aircraft flew in this role for 20 years until retired at Lasham, Hampshire, in the United Kingdom, where it still resides in a derelict state.

Aero Zambia was briefly the national carrier for the country, operating a small fleet of Boeing 737-200s until it was closed down in January 2000. This example is 9J-AFW, the 72nd 737 built and originally ordered by Wien Consolidated Airlines in Alaska – a forerunner of Alaska Airlines.

Here, the same aircraft is seen in 1998 being flown by the short-lived South African airline Interair, which leased it from Aero Zambia. It was common for older airliners to find their way to developing countries in Africa for the final years of their life. The aircraft was retired in 2005.

An Air Sinai Boeing 737-266 powers out of Cairo in 1988 on a flight to Tel Aviv. This airline was a subsidiary of EgyptAir set up to operate flights between Egypt and Israel to satisfy the political issues surrounding the Egypt-Israel peace treaty of 1979. The aircraft was leased from EgyptAir between 1983 and 1990.

A former Aer Lingus machine built in 1979, this 737-200 spent the final ten years of its active life on lease to Kenya Airways for operations on domestic and regional routes, between 1998 and 2008 when it was grounded. In 2001, the airframe was one of 73 abandoned aircraft auctioned off by Nairobi Airport. The buyer later removed it with the intention of turning it into a tourist hotel.

Tunisia's national airline Tunisair leased this 737-2Q9 from Trans European Airways in 1988, according to the Belgian registration of the aircraft. Tunisair had its own fleet of four 737-200s in the 2000s but had leased many examples from other carriers since the first arrived in 1978.

Tunisair founded Tuninter in 1980 to act as a domestic airline, eventually expanding to include international flights. It was renamed SevenAir in 2007, and later Tunisair Express, before merging into the mainline carrier in 2016. This 737-2H6 started life with Malaysian Airline System in 1986 and joined Tuninter in 1998 for three years before moving on. It was written-off in Indonesia in 2008.

Perhaps the most well-known Boeing 737-200s in the world today are those still owned by Air Zimbabwe. The carrier, which took delivery of three of the type in 1986, has kept at least two of them active right up until recent times as financial troubles in the country have prevented the acquisition of newer aircraft. This example, Z-WPA, was the first to arrive and is seen here in 2003. Its career, serving domestic and African destinations from its home base at Harare, saw it still active in late 2022 and it may possibly be flown again should the need arise.

Air Mali, based at Bamako, acquired a single 737-2D6 from Air Algérie in 1982. This aircraft, TZ-ADL, flew on regional services across Africa alongside the airline's 707-300 and 727-200 aircraft, which were used on longer distance services. This 737 moved on to Britannia Airways in 1986.

The Boeing 737-200 was the first jet aircraft equipment used by Air Namibia, introduced in 1989. A total of nine examples were leased over the years, with this – V5-ANA – being one of the longest serving. It was leased from Safair in South Africa between 1991 and 2006, despite the airline being nearly 50 years old at this point.

Right: ZS-NNG was one of the many 737-236s operated by British Airways. Bought by Comair in 1995, it flew in South Africa for 16 years before moving on again to Bhoja Air in Pakistan. Comair had a long-term franchise agreement with British Airways, so was a natural outlet for these aircraft when retired from the UK. The final example flew with the airline in 2010. (Robbie Shaw)

Below: Mediterranean Air Service was a regional airline from Tunisia. It leased this 737-200, TS-IOD, from Tunisair between 1999 and 2001.

Iraqi Airways was a customer of the Boeing 737-200 from the 1970s with a fleet of three Combi variants. However, the airline suffered years of grounding in the 1990s and early 2000s following conflicts in the country and the imposition of no-fly zones in its airspace. By the time flights were launched again in the mid-2000s, the original fleet had been disposed of and a number of leased 737s were brought in. This example wears the registration of owner Teebah Airlines of Sierra Leone. However, it would soon be re-registered YI-APW.

Gulf Air became an independent, albeit government-owned, carrier in 1973, having previously been known as Gulf Aviation since its founding in 1950. It immediately began a period of growth, adding new routes, high-capacity Lockheed L-1011 TriStar aircraft, and a fleet of Boeing 737-200s. This example, A4O-BH, arrived straight from the manufacturer in 1978 and continued with the airline until 1994. It later flew for COPA Airlines in Panama.

Saudi Arabia's national airline introduced the first of 26 Boeing 737-200s in 1972, shortly after it rebranded as Saudia. This example, HZ-AGR, flew with the airline until 2006. Prior to their introduction, Saudia's fleet had comprised older piston airliners for short and regional routes, alongside larger aircraft including the Boeing 707. The 737 marked the start of a period of modernisation and growth for the airline.

Prior to the Iranian Revolution in 1979, the country was a frequent customer of Boeing aircraft for both its national airline and government fleet. This Boeing 737-286 was delivered in 1977 and is still part of the active fleet today, but it is rarely seen flying.

Chapter 9

Boeing 737 -100 and -200 Today

Following a 20-year production run, the final 737-200 was delivered in 1988 and most of the thousand plus airframes have slowly been withdrawn from use and ultimately scrapped. The final airframe, with line number 1,585, was delivered to Xiamen Airlines.

Despite a slow start, persistence paid off for Boeing, with the 737-200 eventually becoming a bestseller and even surpassing the 727, which was somewhat a golden child.

Successive variants of 737 have kept Boeing busy ever since. The follow-up 737-300, -400 and -500 models through the 1980s and early 90s, the Next Generation models of the late 1990s and early 2000s, and today's 737 MAX range continuing to sell extremely well thanks to continual advances in the design, technology, economies and comfort onboard. What made the 737 popular when first introduced, is still largely what attracts airlines from a variety of background and business models today. Combined sales across all variants are now well over 10,000 aircraft.

There are no 737-100s left flying today, and only one known to exist in the form of the prototype at the Museum of Flight in Seattle. However, the 737-200 does remain in active service, and a number survive in preservation.

By far the largest concentration of active 737-200s is in Canada. The aircraft's ability to operate from gravel runways, with the special kits to protect the fuselage and engines from loose debris, means airlines Air Inuit, Canadian North, Chrono Aviation and Nolinor Aviation can use these aircraft to serve communities and mining operations in the remote north of the country.

These aircraft are mostly Combi variants, which can carry a mixture of passengers and cargo, with a movable bulkhead to adapt the size of either cabin to suit their daily needs. C-GNLK, a 737-2K2C, is at present the oldest active Boeing 737 in the world and flies for Nolinor out of its Montreal base. It first flew in 1974.

The 737s operated in Canada have been maintained and upgraded meticulously over the years to enable them to continue in this role. However, they will ultimately be retired in favour of younger replacements over coming years.

In the US, Ameristar Jet Charter has a single 737-200 in passenger configuration, used on VIP charter flights. Above (Jean-Philippe Richard/CC3 via Wikimedia Commons) and Below (Quintin Soloviev/CC4 via Wikimedia Commons)

South America remains a hot spot for active 737-200 airframes, with examples flying for a number of cargo and military operators such as the Ecuadorian Air Force and Bolovian Air Force. In Venezuela, no fewer than four operators are still flying seven examples of these now vintage aircraft, including RUTACA Airlines, Venezolana, Estelar Latinoamerica, and Avior Airlines. This example, with a very smart livery, is flying for cargo carrier Aerosucre of Colombia. (Felipe Betancur)

In the Middle East, the Indian Air Force still has two 737-200s in active service. These were formerly commercial aircraft operated by Indian Airlines and are now used for VIP transport roles. (Sean DSilva)

Iran was also a bastion of the 737, owing to the sanctions in place that prevent its airlines from acquiring new aircraft or parts. Although no passenger examples now remain in service, there are still 737-200s flown by the government of Iran, and some preserved examples at the Aerospace Exhibition in Tehran. (Mehrad Watson)

Indonesia, which saw the last of the world's great 737-200 fleets in the 1990s and early 2000s, has no passenger carriers operating the type today. However, some of its cargo airlines still fly the venerable jet. My Indo Airlines is one example, and the Indonesian Air Force also has active -200s.

This former Dan-Air London machine has found its way miraculously into a quarry in south Bali, where plans were being formed for it to become a tourist attraction.

Above, below and opposite: In the Philippines, SEAIR International is a cargo carrier based at Clark. It uses two 737-200C freighters, which still fly regularly on domestic hops around the country. (Dirk Grothe)

Finally, in Africa, there are still various small carriers and private operators using the 737-200 on cargo and VIP services. In the Democratic Republic of Congo, a government aircraft, 9T-TCQ, is active. Transafrican Air of Kenya has a single 737-290C freighter active. Meanwhile, Halla Airlines, also of Kenya, is still thought to be flying this aircraft in passenger configuration. (James Ralph)

Boeing 737-281 HS-AKO, which once flew for the likes of All Nippon Airways, Sempati Air and Phuket Air, now wears a false AirAsia livery in its new role as part of the Kidzania attraction in Bangkok. (Dirk Grothe)

Most of the world's 737-200 fleets were retired and scrapped with no resale, given the high number of hours they had achieved, particularly those used on mainline trunk services in the employ of airlines across the Americas and Europe. There are, however, many retired 737-200s still sitting idle at airports around the world, unlikely to ever fly again.

Thankfully, a number of 737-200s have also found their way into preservation at museums and training institutions around the world. Some are complete, whilst others survive as cockpits or forward fuselage sections. The forward fuselage of this former USAir and Piedmont example is on display at the Museum of Flight in Seattle.

Chapter 10

Technical Specifications

Boeing saw the potential for the 737 to be used in less developed surroundings by airlines operating from unprepared airstrips made of grass, dirt or even gravel. In fact, the prototype demonstrated its ability to land and take-off from a grass runway at Hope Regional Airpark in British Colombia in September 1972.
One feature offered was the so-called 'gravel kit', which could be fitted to the nosewheel to deflect any debris from being thrown up and causing damage to the fuselage. Smaller deflectors were also added to the main gear to protect the wings and flaps, and vortex deflectors protruding from the front of the engines prevented debris from being ingested.
A gravel kit is seen here on RP-C4753 at Cebu in the Philippines in 2023. (Dirk Grothe)

Boeing 737-100

Engines	2 x P&W JT8D-7, JT8D-9 or JT8D-15/15A
Span	28.3m (93ft)
Length	28.65m (94ft)
Height	11.23m (36ft 10in)
Wing Area	102m² (1,098sq ft)
Max Take-Off Weight	49,940kg (110,000lb)
Max Landing Weight	46,720kg (103,000lb)
Max Payload	103 passengers
Max Cruising Speed	869kph (540mph)
Range With Full Load	2,850km (1,540mi)
Ceiling	11,300m (37,000ft)
First Operator	Lufthansa

Boeing 737-200/200C/200QC

Engines	2 x P&W JT8D-9A, JT8D-15/15A or JT8D-17/17A
Span	28.3m (93ft)
Length	30.53m (100ft 2in)
Height	11.22m (36ft 10in)
Wing Area	102m² (1,098sq ft)
Max Take-Off Weight	52,437kg (115,500lb)
Max Landing Weight	46,720kg (103,000lb)
Max Payload	130 passengers
Max Cruising Speed	869kph (540mph)
Range With Full Load	3,435km (2,600mi)
Ceiling	11,300m (37,000ft)
First Operator	United Airlines

Boeing 737-200 Advanced

Engines	2 x P&W JT8D-9A, JT8D-15/15A or JT8D-17/17A
Span	28.3m (93ft)
Length	30.53m (100ft 2in)
Height	11.22m (36ft 10in)
Wing Area	102m² (1,098sq ft)
Max Take-Off Weight	58,157kg (128,100lb)
Max Landing Weight	48,534kg (107,000lb)
Max Payload	130 passengers
Max Cruising Speed	869kph (540mph)
Range With Full Load	4,256km (2,645mi)
Ceiling	11,300m (37,000ft)
First Operator	All Nippon Airways

Bibliography

Shaw, R., *Boeing 737-100/-200*, Airlife Publishing Ltd, 2001

Halford-Macleod, G., *Britain's Airlines: 1964 to Deregulation*, History Press, 2010

Simons, G. M., *Britannia Airways: The World's Largest Holiday Airline Air World*, 2020

Swanborough, G., *Civil Aircraft of the World*; Ian Allan Ltd, 1972

Cartledge, M., *Flying Firsts*, Destinworld Publishing Ltd, 2018

Ott. J., *Jets: Airliners of the Golden Age*, Airlife Publishing Ltd, 1993

Green, W., Swanborough, G., Mowinski J., *Modern Commercial Aircraft*, Salamander Books, 1988

Halford-Macleod, G., *Telling Aircraft Tails*, History Press, 2021

Other books you might like:

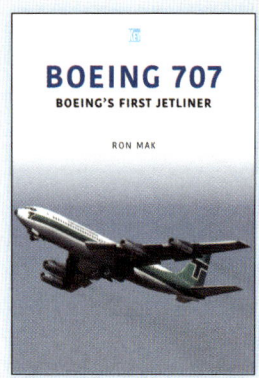
Historic Commercial Aircraft Series, Vol. 2

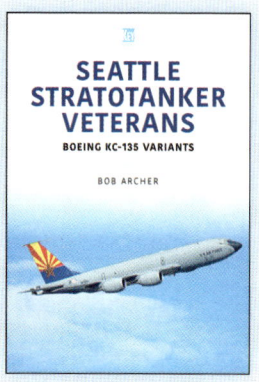
Modern Military Aircraft Series, Vol. 11

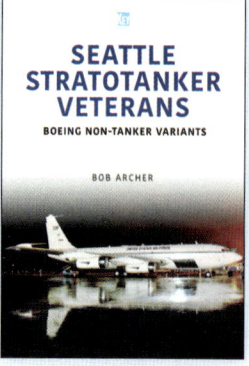
Modern Military Aircraft Series, Vol. 12

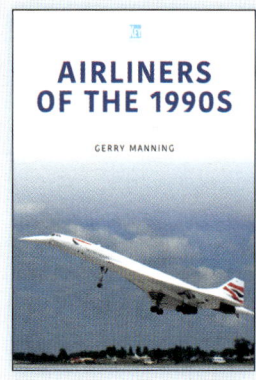
Historic Commercial Aircraft Series, Vol. 4

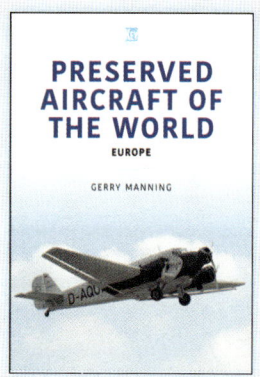
Preserved Aircraft of the World

Historic Commercial Aircraft Series, Vol. 5

For our full range of titles please visit:
shop.keypublishing.com/books

VIP Book Club

Sign up today and receive
TWO FREE E-BOOKS

Be the first to find out about our forthcoming book releases and receive exclusive offers.

Register now at **keypublishing.com/vip-book-club**

Our VIP Book Club is a 100% spam-free zone, and we will never share your email with anyone else. You can read our full privacy policy at: privacy.keypublishing.com